Better Guitar With..

Rockschool

www.rockschool.co.uk

Welcome To Guitar Grade 1

Welcome to the Rockschool Guitar Grade 1 pack. The book and CD contain everything needed to play guitar in this grade. In the book you will find the exam scores in both standard guitar notation and TAB. The accompanying CD has full stereo mixes of each tune, backing tracks to play along with for practice, tuning notes and spoken two bar count-ins to each piece. Handy tips on playing the pieces and the marking schemes can be found in the Guru's Guide on page 16. If you have any queries about this or any other Rockschool exam, please call us on **0845 460 4747**, email us at *info@rockschool.co.uk* or visit our website *www.rockschool.co.uk*. Good luck!

Level 1 Requirements for Grades 1, 2 & 3

The nine Rockschool grades are divided into four levels. These levels correspond to the levels of the National Qualifications Framework (NQF). Further details about the NQF can be found at *www.qca.org.uk/NQF*. Details of all Rockschool's accredited qualifications can be found at *www.qca.org.uk/openquals*.

Guitar Grade 1 is part of Level 1. This Level is for players who are just starting out and who are looking to build a solid technical and stylistic foundation for their playing.

Grade 1: a player of Grade 1 standard should be able to play up to 32 bars of music using first position chords and melodies composed of whole, half, quarter and eighth notes and associated rests, tied notes, and dotted half and quarter notes. Performances should include basic legato and staccato playing where marked.

Grade 2: in this grade you are beginning to acquire a range of physical and expressive techniques, including palm muting and the use of double stops on adjacent strings, simple legato and staccato and slides, as well as simple dynamics. In this grade you will also begin to work on your stylistic appreciation.

Grade 3: this grade continues the foundation work started in Grade 2. As a player you will be encountering syncopated eighth and sixteenth note strumming as well as developing the palette of expressive techniques to include fretting hand and whammy bar vibrato, hammer ons and pull offs, slides and simple bends. The pieces of music are now longer, covering two pages and you should be developing your stylistic awareness, taking into account amp settings for each song.

Guitar Exams at Grade 1

There are **two** types of exam that can be taken using this pack: a Grade Exam and a Performance Certificate.

Guitar Grade 1 Exam: this is for players who want to develop performance and technical skills

Players wishing to enter for a Guitar Grade 1 exam need to prepare **three** pieces of which **one** may be a free choice piece chosen from outside the printed repertoire. In addition you must prepare the technical exercises in the book, undertake either a sight reading test or an improvisation & interpretation test, take an ear test and answer general musicianship questions. Samples of these tests are printed in the book along with audio examples on the CD.

Guitar Grade 1 Performance Certificate: this is for players who want to focus on performing in a range of styles

To enter for your Guitar Grade 1 Performance Certificate you play pieces only. You can choose any **five** of the six tunes printed in this book, or you can choose to bring in up to **two** free choice pieces as long as they meet the standards set out by Rockschool. Free choice piece checklists for all grades can be found on the Rockschool website: *www.rockschool.co.uk*.

Guitar Notation Explained

THE MUSICAL STAVE shows pitches and rhythms and is divided by lines into bars. Pitches are named after the first seven letters of the alphabet.

TABLATURE graphically represents the guitar fingerboard. Each horizontal line represents a string, and each number represents a fret.

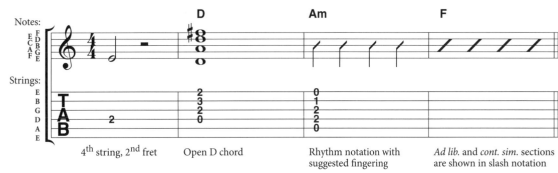

4th string, 2nd fret   Open D chord   Rhythm notation with suggested fingering   *Ad lib.* and *cont. sim.* sections are shown in slash notation

Definitions For Special Guitar Notation

HAMMER ON: Pick the lower note, then sound the higher note by fretting it without picking.

PULL OFF: Pick the higher note then sound the lower note by lifting the finger without picking.

SLIDE: Pick the first note, then slide to the next with the same finger.

STRING BENDS: Pick the first note then bend (or release the bend) to the pitch indicated in brackets.

GLISSANDO: A small slide off of a note toward the end of its rhythmic duration. Do not slide 'into' the following note – subsequent notes should be repicked.

VIBRATO: Vibrate the note by bending and releasing the string smoothly and continuously.

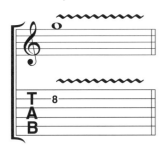

TRILL: Rapidly alternate between the two bracketed notes by hammering on and pulling off.

NATURAL HARMONICS: Lightly touch the string above the indicated fret then pick to sound a harmonic.

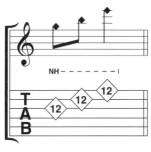

PINCHED HARMONICS: Bring the thumb of the picking hand into contact with the string immediately after the pick.

PICK HAND TAP: Strike the indicated note with a finger from the picking hand. Usually followed by a pull off.

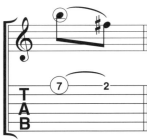

FRET HAND TAP: As pick hand tap, but use fretting hand. Usually followed by a pull off or hammer on.

QUARTER TONE BEND: Pick the note indicated and bend the string up by a quarter tone.

PRE-BENDS: Before picking the note, bend the string from the fret indicated between the staves, to the equivalent pitch indicated in brackets in the TAB

WHAMMY BAR BEND: Use the whammy bar to bend notes to the pitches indicated in brackets in the TAB

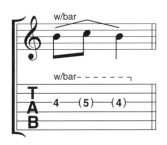

D.%. al Coda

D.C. al Fine

- Go back to the sign (%), then play until the bar marked *To Coda* ⊕ then skip to the section marked ⊕ *Coda*.

- Go back to the beginning of the song and play until the bar marked *Fine* (end).

- Repeat bars between signs.

- When a repeated section has different endings, play the first ending only the first time and the second ending only the second time.

Gone But Not Forgotten

Deirdre Cartwright

Head On

Hussein Boon

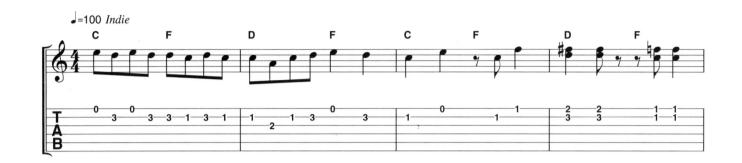

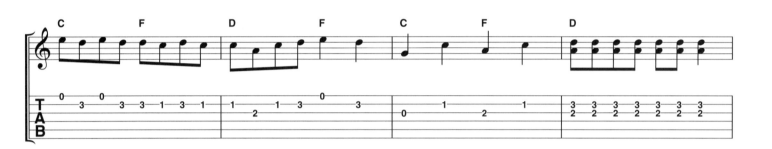

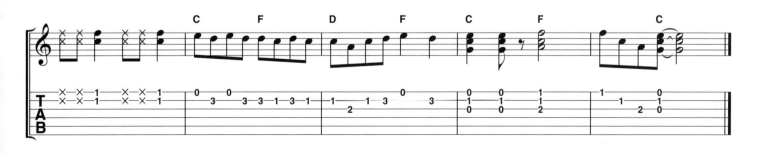

Gotta Lotta Rosa

Joe Bennett

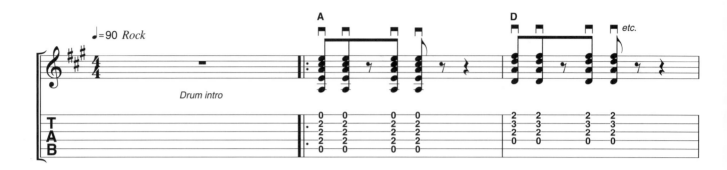

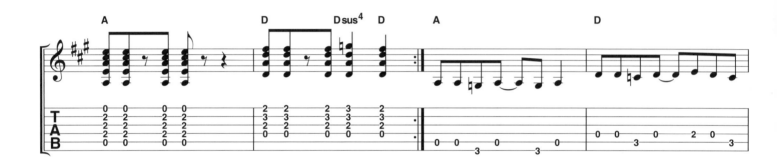

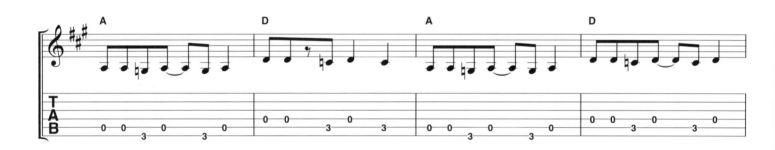

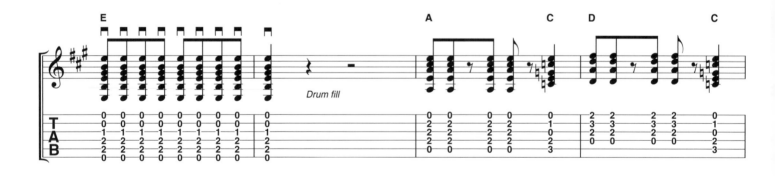

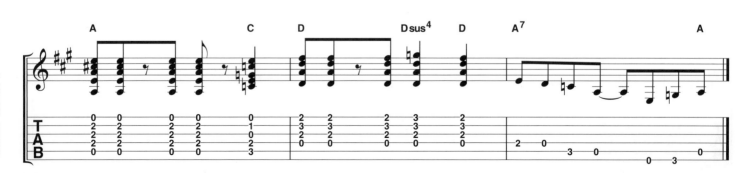

Jazz Trip

Finbar Josephs

Hey Jack

Deirdre Cartwright

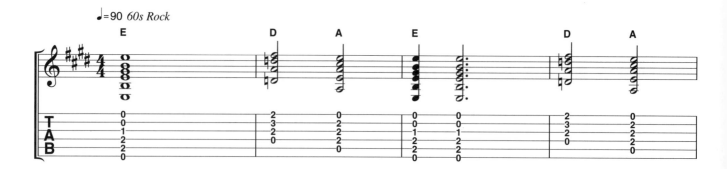

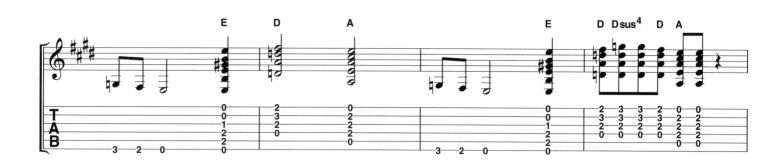

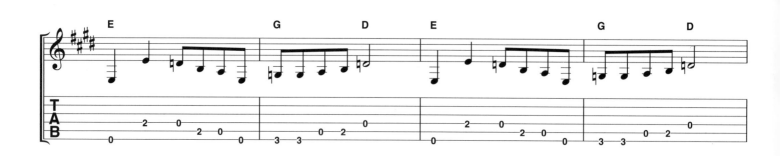

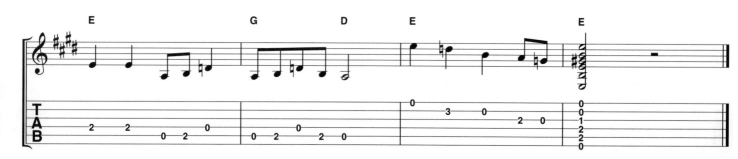

© 2006 Rock School Ltd.

Ruff And Smooth

Adrian York

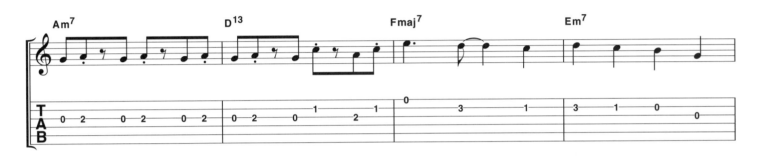

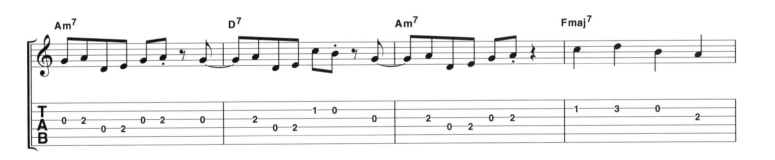

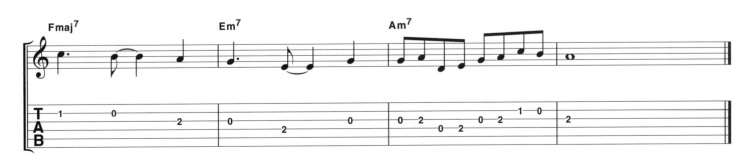

Guitar Grade 1

Technical Exercises

In this section, the examiner will ask you to play a selection of exercises drawn from each of the three groups shown below. Groups A and B contain examples of the kinds of scales and chords you can use when playing the pieces. In Group C you will be asked to prepare the exercise and play it to the CD backing track. You do not need to memorise the exercises (and can use the book in the exam) but the examiner will be looking for the speed of your response. The examiner will also give credit for the level of your musicality.

Groups A and B should be prepared in the keys directed.
Groups A and B should be played at ♩ = 80. The examiner will give you this tempo in the exam.

Group A: Scales

1. C major scale

2. A natural minor scale

3. Minor pentatonic scale to be prepared in E and A. E minor pentatonic shown

Group B: Chords

1. Power chords. The power chords shown below should be played as a continuous exercise

Grade Exam and Performance Certificate Entry Form

Please complete the form below in BLOCK CAPITALS. Information given below will only be used by Rockschool for exam purposes and for Rockschool news. Completed application forms should be sent, along with a cheque made payable to 'Rockschool' for the appropriate fees, to:

Exam Entries, Rockschool, Evergreen House, 2-4 King Street, Twickenham, Middlesex, TW1 3RZ

1. Candidate's Details

Full Name (as it will appear on the certificate):

Date of Birth (DD/MM/YY)*:   Gender (M/F)*:   *This information is compulsory but will be used for statistical purposes only

Address:

                          Postcode:

Telephone No: Mobile No:

Email address:

☐ (Please tick) **Yes!** I would like to receive all correspondence from Rockschool via email (with the exception of certificates and mark sheets which will be posted). *Rockschool will NOT circulate your email address to any third parties.*

2. Your Examination

Type of Exam (Grade or Performance Certificate):   Grade:

Instrument: *If you are applying for multiple examinations, please continue below:*

Type of Exam:	Instrument:	Grade:
Type of Exam:	Instrument:	Grade:

Period (A/B/C)*:   *Refer to our website for exam periods and closing dates*

Preferred Town for Examination (*Refer to our website for a list of current towns with Rockschool examination centres**):

         Rockschool will endeavour to place you at your preferred town, but cannot guarantee this

Please state any dates that are IMPOSSIBLE for you to attend*:

         It is not guaranteed that we can avoid these dates

3. Additional information

Drum Candidates. Do you require a left-handed kit?

Will you be bringing your own kit (Grades 6,7,8 only)?   If 'no' Rockschool will provide a drum kit.

Popular Piano Candidates. Will you be bringing your own keyboard?

If 'no', Rockschool can provide either a keyboard or a piano. Please indicate which you prefer :

Special Needs Candidates. Please include a supporting letter with your application explaining your requirements.

All Candidates. If there is any additional information you consider relevant, please attach a note to your application.

4. Fees — *For current exam prices please refer to our website, www.rockschool.co.uk or call us on 0845 460 4747*

Fee enclosed:

Cheque Number: PLEASE WRITE CANDIDATE NAME ON BACK OF CHEQUE

ROCKSCHOOL HELPLINE: 0845 460 4747

email: info@rockschool.co.uk   website: www.rockschool.co.uk

rockschool

Teacher's Exam Entry Form

Teachers wishing to enter **grade exams** and **performance certificates** on behalf of their students should complete the form below in BLOCK CAPITALS. Information given will only be used by Rockschool for exam purposes and for Rockschool news. You can get up to date information on examination prices from **www.rockschool.co.uk** or by ringing the Rockschool helpline on **0845 460 4747**. Completed application forms should be sent, along with a cheque made payable to **'Rockschool'** for the appropriate fees, to:

Exam Entries, Rockschool, Evergreen House, 2-4 King Street, Twickenham, Middlesex, TW1 3RZ

1. Teacher's Details

Title (Mr/Mrs/Ms etc):   Full Name:

Address:

                                                              Postcode:

Telephone No: Mobile No:

Email address:

For school entries please include your NCN (National Centre Number):

☐ (Please tick) **Yes!** I would like to receive all correspondence from Rockschool via email (with the exception of certificates and mark sheets which will be posted). *Rockschool will NOT circulate your email address to any third parties.*

2. Examination Details and Fees

*For grade exams, please write '**G**' and the grade number in the Grade box (e.g. **G6** for Grade 6). For performance certificates, please write '**PC**' and the grade number in the Grade box (e.g. **PC4** for Performance Certificate Grade 4). †For examination periods refer to our website. Continue on separate sheet if necessary.*

FOR SPECIAL NEEDS CANDIDATES PLEASE ATTACH A SUPPORTING LETTER WITH DETAILS.

Candidate's Name (as it will appear on the certificate)	Date of Birth	Gender (M/F)	Instrument	Grade*	Period†	Fee (£)
1.	DD MM YYYY					
2.	DD MM YYYY					
3.	DD MM YYYY					
4.	DD MM YYYY					
5.	DD MM YYYY					
6.	DD MM YYYY					
7.	DD MM YYYY					
8.	DD MM YYYY					
9.	DD MM YYYY					
10.	DD MM YYYY					
11.	DD MM YYYY					
12.	DD MM YYYY					
				Total fees enclosed £		

Preferred Town for Examination (*Refer to our website for a list of current towns with Rockschool examination centres**):

*Rockschool will endeavour to place your candidates at your preferred town, but cannot guarantee this

Please list dates your candidate(s) **cannot** attend*:

*It is not guaranteed that we can avoid these dates

Band Exam Entry Form

You can enter for one of the following band exams (1 Guitar player, 1 Bass player, 1 Drummer) using Rockschool materials: *** Level One (Grade 3 repertoire) * Level Two (Grade 5 repertoire) *Level Three (Grade 8 repertoire)** Please complete the form below in BLOCK CAPITALS. Information given will only be used by Rockschool for exam purposes and for Rockschool news. Completed application forms should be sent, along with a cheque made payable to **'Rockschool'** for the appropriate fees, to:

Exam Entries, Rockschool, Evergreen House, 2-4 King Street, Twickenham, Middlesex, TW1 3RZ

1. Band's Details

GUITARIST Full Name (as it will appear on the certificate):

Date of Birth (DD/MM/YY)*:   Gender (M/F)*:

BASSIST Full Name (as it will appear on the certificate):

Date of Birth (DD/MM/YY)*:   Gender (M/F)*:

DRUMMER Full Name (as it will appear on the certificate):

Date of Birth (DD/MM/YY)*:   Gender (M/F)*:

*This information is compulsory but will be used for statistical purposes only

2. Band's Main Contact Details

Main Contact's Name:

Address:

Postcode:

Telephone No: Mobile No:

Email address:

☐ (Please tick) **Yes!** I would like to receive all correspondence from Rockschool via email (with the exception of certificates and mark sheets which will be posted). *Rockschool will NOT circulate your email address to any third parties.*

3. Your Examination — *If you are applying for multiple exams, please use a separate form for each*

Exam Level (One/Two/Three):

Period (A/B/C)*:   *Refer to our website for exam periods and closing dates*

Preferred Town for Examination (*Refer to our website for a list of current towns with Rockschool examination centres**):

Rockschool will endeavour to place you at your preferred town, but cannot guarantee this

Please state any dates that are IMPOSSIBLE for you to attend*:

*It is not guaranteed that we can avoid these dates

Additional Information *If there is any additional information you consider relevant (e.g. band members with special needs) please attach a separate sheet explaining your requirements.*

4. Fees — *For current exam prices please refer to our website,* **www.rockschool.co.uk** *or call us on* **0845 460 4747**

Fee enclosed:

Cheque Number: PLEASE WRITE CANDIDATES' NAMES ON BACK OF CHEQUE

ROCKSCHOOL HELPLINE: 0845 460 4747
email: info@rockschool.co.uk   website: www.rockschool.co.uk

ROCKSCHOOL RESOURCES

At Rockschool we recognise the importance of keeping teachers and learners up to date with developments. Below are listed the qualifications and resources on offer. If you have any questions, please contact us through the relevant email address, or phone us on **0845 460 4747**.

PERFORMANCE DIPLOMAS

Music Performance Diploma
(DipRSL Perf) at Level 4

Music Performance Licentiate
(LRSL Perf) at Level 6

The Rockschool Performance Diplomas provide flexible, vocationally relevant qualifications for experienced or skilled performers of popular music.

diplomas@rockschool.co.uk

TEACHING DIPLOMAS

Teaching Diploma
(DipRSL) at Level 4
Teaching Diploma
(LRSL) at Level 6

The Rockschool Teaching Diplomas have been devised for instrumentalists, vocalists and music technologists who would like to attain a teaching qualification without having to attend a course or write essays. The diplomas focus on the practicalities of teaching and are neither genre nor instrument specific.

diplomas@rockschool.co.uk

MUSIC PRACTITIONERS QUALIFICATIONS

Rockschool/ATM
14-19 Diploma
Compatible

These flexible, vocationally relevant popular music qualifications will provide learners with the necessary skills to develop realistic employment opportunities in the music industry.

qualifications@rockschool.co.uk

COMPANION GUIDES

Sight Reading (Grades 1-8)
Improvisation & Interpretation
(Grades 1-5)
QSPs (Grades 6-8)
Ear Tests (Grades 1-8)
GMQs (Grades 1-8)

A must for any music teacher or self-taught musician using the Rockschool grade system. Rockschool Companion Guides contain examples of the exercises you will encounter in an exam along with tips on how best to perform.

info@rockschool.co.uk

Companion Guides available for purchase through **www.musicroom.com**

GUITAR DVDS

Following DVDs available:
Grades Debut & 1
Grade 2
Grade 3

Perfect for anyone working through the Rockschool grades, Rockschool DVDs include instructional lessons on how to make the most of the pieces and technical exercises required in your exams.

info@rockschool.co.uk

DVDs available for purchase through **www.musicroom.com**

COMING SOON...REPERTOIRE BOOKS

Rockschool Repertoire Books contain popular songs from rock through to indie. **Drums Grades 1 to 3** will be available from October 2008.

info@rockschool.co.uk

Repertoire Books soon available for purchase through **www.musicroom.com**

2. Major chords.

3. Minor chords

Group C: Riff

In the exam you will be asked to play the following riff to the backing track on the CD. The riff shown in bar 1 should be played in the same shape in bars 2–4. The root note of the pattern to be played is shown in the music in each of the subsequent three bars. The tempo is ♩ = 70.

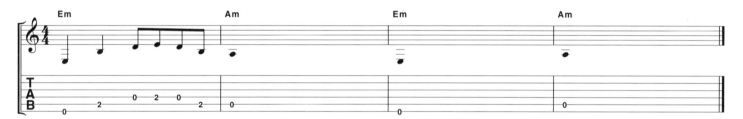

Sight Reading

In this section you have a choice between **either** a sight reading test **or** an improvisation & interpretation test (see facing page). Printed below is the type of sight reading test you are likely to encounter in the exam. The piece will be composed in the style of either rock or blues. The examiner will allow you 90 seconds to prepare it and will set the tempo for you on a metronome. The tempo is ♩=60.

Improvisation & Interpretation

Printed below is an example of the type of improvisation & interpretation test you are likely to encounter in the exam. You will be asked to play an improvised line to a backing track lasting four bars in the style of rock or blues. You may choose to play either rhythmic chords or a melodic lead line. You will be allowed 30 seconds to prepare. You will be allowed to practise through one playing of the test on the CD before playing it a second time for the exam. This test is continuous with a one bar count in at the beginning and after the practice session. The tempo is ♩ = 60.

Ear Tests

There are two ear tests in this grade. The examiner will play each test to you on CD. You will find one example of each type of test you will be given in the exam printed below.

Test 1: Melodic Recall

You will be asked to play back on your guitar a simple melody of not more than two bars composed from the first three notes of the C major scale (C, D and E). You will be given the tonic note and told the starting note and you will hear the test twice with a drum backing. There will then be a short break for you to practise the test and then the test will recommence. You will play the melody with the drum backing. This test is continuous. The tempo is ♩=90.

Test 2: Rhythmic Recall

You will be asked to play back the given two bar rhythm on the open bottom E string of your guitar. You will hear the rhythm played twice with a drum backing. There will then be a short break for you to practise the test and then the test will recommence and you will play the rhythm to the drum backing. This test is continuous. The tempo is ♩=90.

General Musicianship Questions

You will be asked five General Musicianship Questions at the end of the exam. The examiner will ask questions based on pieces you have played in the exam. Some of the theoretical topics can be found in the Technical Exercises.

Topics:

i)   Music theory
ii)   Knowledge of your instrument

The music theory questions will cover the recognition of the following at this grade:

Note pitches
Note values
Rests
Time Signatures
Notes on the stave

Knowledge of the difference between the following chord types:

Major
Minor

The instrument knowledge questions will cover the following topics at this grade:

Plugging into the amplifier and the guitar
Volume and tone adjustments on the guitar
Knowledge of open string note names

Knowledge of parts of the guitar:

Fretboard, neck, body, tuning pegs, nut, pickups, bridge, pickup selectors, scratchplate and jack socket

Questions on all these topics will be based on pieces played by you in the exam. Tips on how to approach this part of the exam can be found in the Rockschool Companion Guide and on the Rockschool website: *www.rockschool.co.uk.*

The Guru's Guide To Guitar Grade 1

This section contains some handy hints compiled by Rockschool's Guitar Guru to help you get the most out of the performance pieces. Do feel free to adapt the tunes to suit your playing style. Remember, these tunes are your chance to show your musical imagination and personality.

The TAB fingerings are suggestions only. Feel free to use different neck positions as they suit you. Please also note that any solos featured in the full mixes are not meant to be indicative of the standard required for the grade.

Guitar Grade 1 Tunes

Rockschool tunes help you play the hit tunes you enjoy. The pieces have been written by top pop and rock composers and players according to style specifications drawn up by Rockschool.

The tunes printed here fall into two categories. The first category can be called the 'contemporary mainstream' and features current styles in today's charts. The second category of pieces consists of 'roots styles', those classic grooves and genres which influence every generation of performers.

CD full mix track 1, backing track 8: Gone But Not Forgotten

This guitar pop track is taken at a brisk pace and combines quite intricate single note work with bold first position chords. The points to watch out for are the change from a chord to single notes in bars 14 and 16 and in the repeated two bar section in bars 17-20. The last chord should be played with a flourish but remember to hold it for two beats only.

Composer: Deirdre Cartwright.

CD full mix track 2, backing track 9: Head On

This is played in an indie style and features a fast flowing opening riff played in eighth notes. The piece mixes up double stops (two notes played together), ties (where one note is held on for a longer time) and some dead notes (where the fingers touch the strings but don't actually sound the notes).

Composer: Hussein Boon.

CD full mix track 3, backing track 10: Gotta Lotta Rosa

This is an unashamedly old fashioned rock song, reminiscent of AC/DC at their best. The opening chords should be played with plenty of attack but make sure that each chord is given its full length and that you play the part evenly. The notation suggests downstrokes only here and towards the end of the piece when the theme is restated.

Composer: Joe Bennett.

CD full mix track 4, backing track 11: Jazz Trip

A modern funk based song that concentrates on melody after a four bar chord introduction. The melody is played in quarter and eighth notes and should be performed evenly. There is one tricky step across two strings at the beginning of bar 10. In the second part of the song, the melody is interspersed with ties, rests and dotted notes.

Composer: Finbar Josephs.

CD full mix track 5, backing track 12: Hey Jack

This 60s rock piece needs to be played with plenty of attack right from the word go. The chords should be bold but not snatched at and remember to count the dotted half notes in the third bar. The single note section in the second half is made up of a repeated, riff-like pattern that is varied towards the end before the final climactic chord.

Composer: Deirdre Cartwright.

CD full mix track 6, backing track 13: Ruff And Smooth

A contemporary R 'n' B track based around a recurring two note riff where the second note is played staccato. The performance of the remainder of the melody should flow effortlessly, taking into account the dotted rhythms and the tied notes which give those sections something of a swing feel to them. The arpeggios in bars 9-11, 16 and 19 need to be picked evenly for full effect.

Composer: Adrian York.

CD Musicians:

Guitar: Deirdre Cartwright; Hussein Boon
Bass: Henry Thomas
Drums: George Gavin
Keyboards and programming: Alastair Gavin

Guitar Grade 1 Marking Schemes

The table below shows the marking scheme for the Guitar Grade 1 exam.

ELEMENT	PASS	MERIT	DISTINCTION
Piece 1	13 out of 20	15 out of 20	17+ out of 20
Piece 2	13 out of 20	15 out of 20	17+ out of 20
Piece 3	13 out of 20	15 out of 20	17+ out of 20
Technical Exercises	11 out of 15	12–13 out of 15	14+ out of 15
Either Sight Reading *or* Improvisation & Interpretation	6 out of 10	7–8 out of 10	9+ out of 10
Ear Tests	6 out of 10	7–8 out of 10	9+ out of 10
General Musicianship Questions	3 out of 5	4 out of 5	5 out of 5
Total Marks	**Pass: 65%+**	**Merit: 75%+**	**Distinction: 85%+**

The table below shows the marking scheme for the Guitar Grade 1 Performance Certificate.

ELEMENT	PASS	MERIT	DISTINCTION
Piece 1	14 out of 20	16 out of 20	18+ out of 20
Piece 2	14 out of 20	16 out of 20	18+ out of 20
Piece 3	14 out of 20	16 out of 20	18+ out of 20
Piece 4	14 out of 20	16 out of 20	18+ out of 20
Piece 5	14 out of 20	16 out of 20	18+ out of 20
Total Marks	**Pass: 70%+**	**Merit: 80%+**	**Distinction: 90%+**

Entering Rockschool Exams

Entering a Rockschool exam is easy. Please read through these instructions carefully before filling in the exam entry form. Information on current exam fees can be obtained from Rockschool by ringing 0845 460 4747 or by logging on to our website *www.rockschool.co.uk.*

• You should enter for your exam when you feel ready.

• You can enter for any one of three examination periods. These are shown below with their closing dates.

PERIOD	DURATION	CLOSING DATE
Period A	1st February to 15th March	1st December
Period B	1st May to 31st July	1st April
Period C	23rd October to 15th December	1st October

These dates will apply from 1st September 2006 until further notice

• Please complete the form giving the information required. Please fill in the type and level of exam, the instrument, along with the period and year. Finally, fill in the fee box with the appropriate amount. You can obtain up to date information on all Rockschool exam fees from the website: *www.rockschool.co.uk.* You should send this form with a cheque or postal order (payable to Rockschool Ltd) to the address shown on the order form. **Please also indicate on the form whether or not you would like to receive notification via email.**

• Applications received after the expiry of the closing date may be accepted subject to the payment of an additional fee.

• When you enter an exam you will receive from Rockschool an acknowledgement letter or email containing a copy of our exam regulations.

• Rockschool will allocate your entry to a centre and you will receive notification of the exam, showing a date, location and time as well as advice of what to bring to the centre. We endeavour to give you four weeks' notice of your exam.

• You should inform Rockschool of any cancellations or alterations to the schedule as soon as you can as it is usually not possible to transfer entries from one centre, or one period, to another without the payment of an additional fee.

• Please bring your music book and CD to the exam. You may not use photocopied music, nor the music used by someone else in another exam. The examiner will sign each book during each examination. You may be barred from taking an exam if you use someone else's music.

• You should aim to arrive for your Grade 1 exam fifteen minutes before the time stated on the schedule.

• Each Grade 1 exam is scheduled to last for 15 minutes. You can use a small proportion of this time to tune up and get ready.

• Two to three weeks after the exam you will receive a copy of the examiner's mark sheet. Every successful player will receive a Rockschool certificate of achievement.